WILD HOR

MW00489907

Adult Coloring Book Of Horses

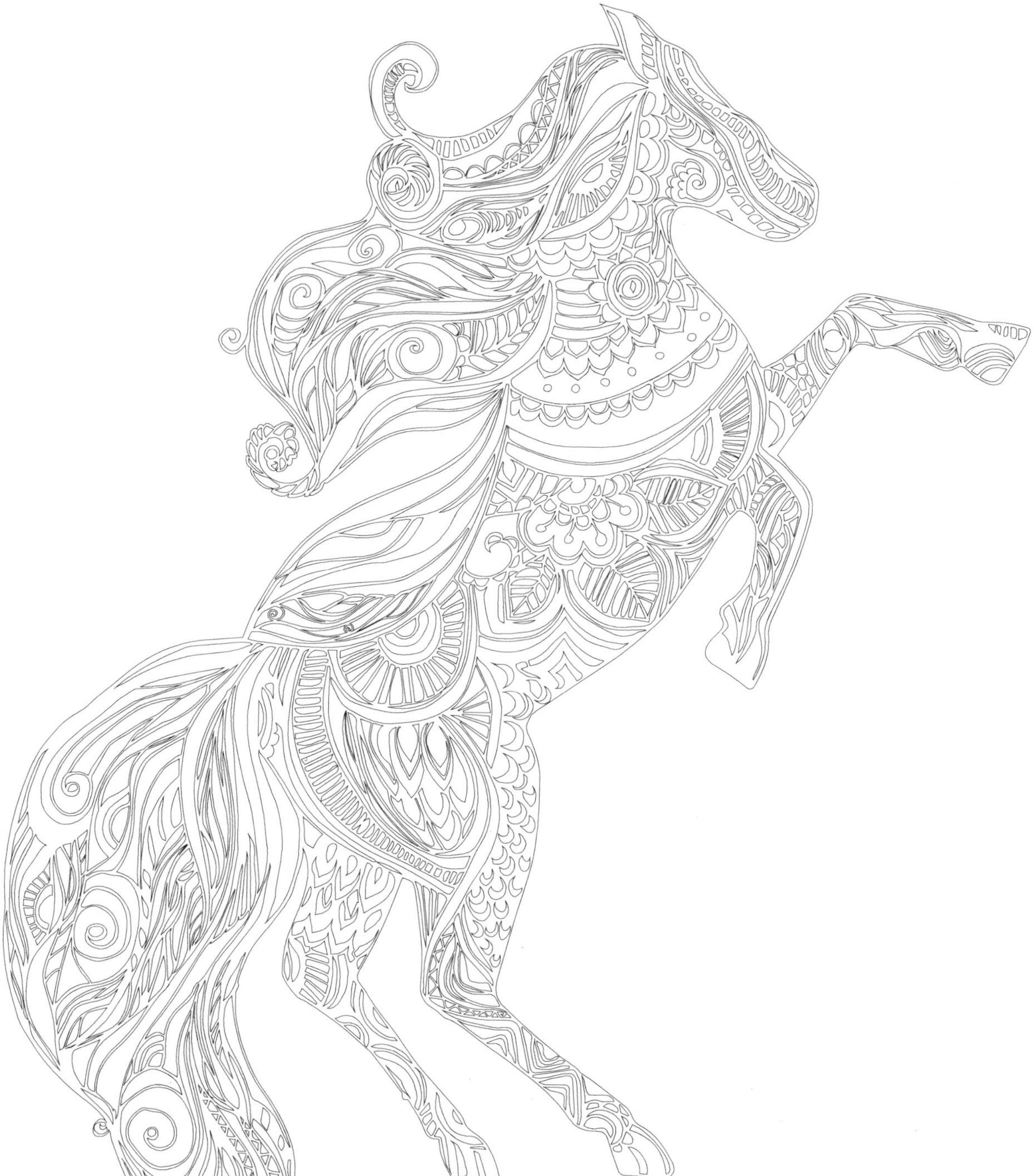

ESPER BOOKS

@COLORING _ ESPER

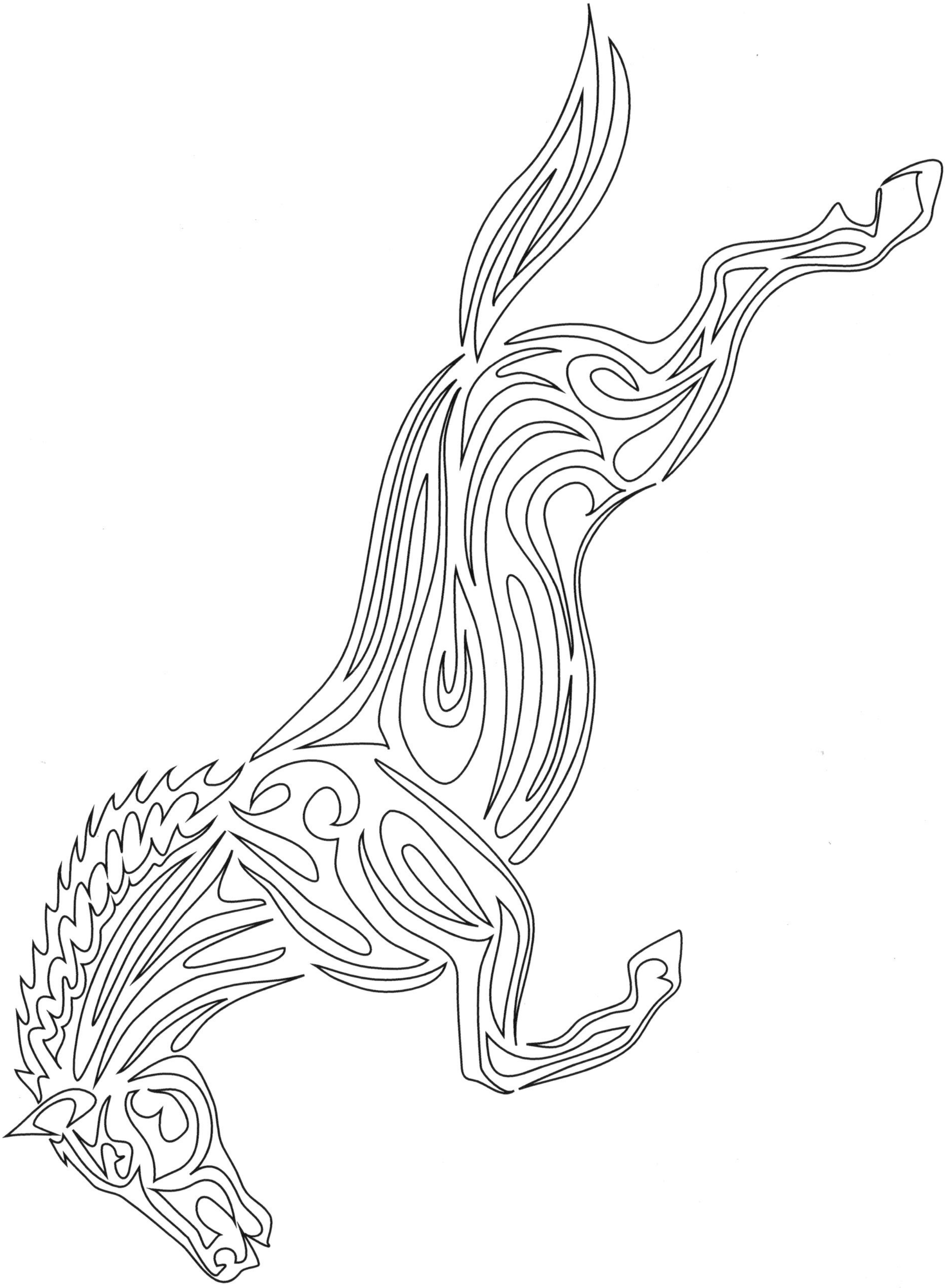

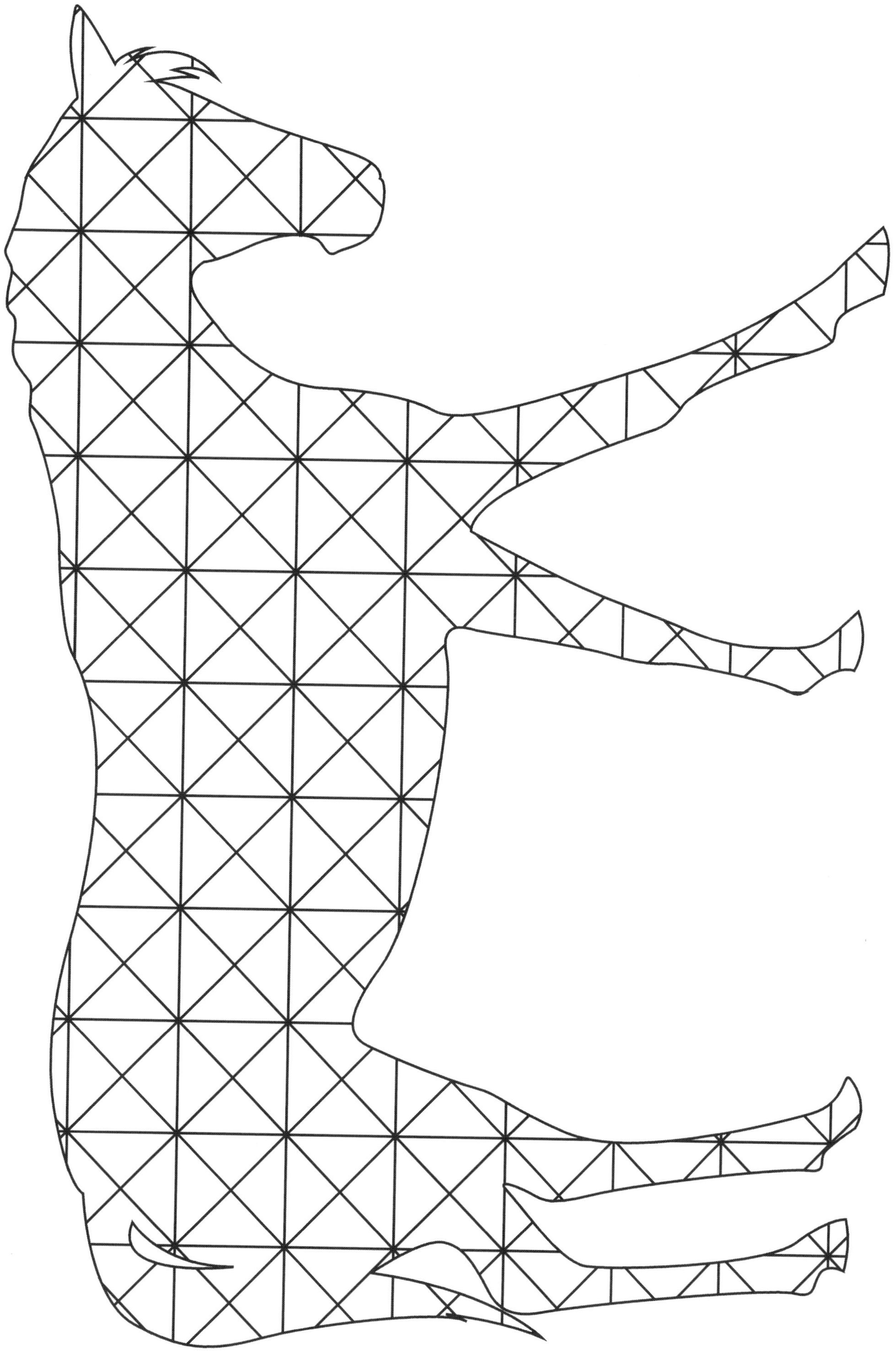

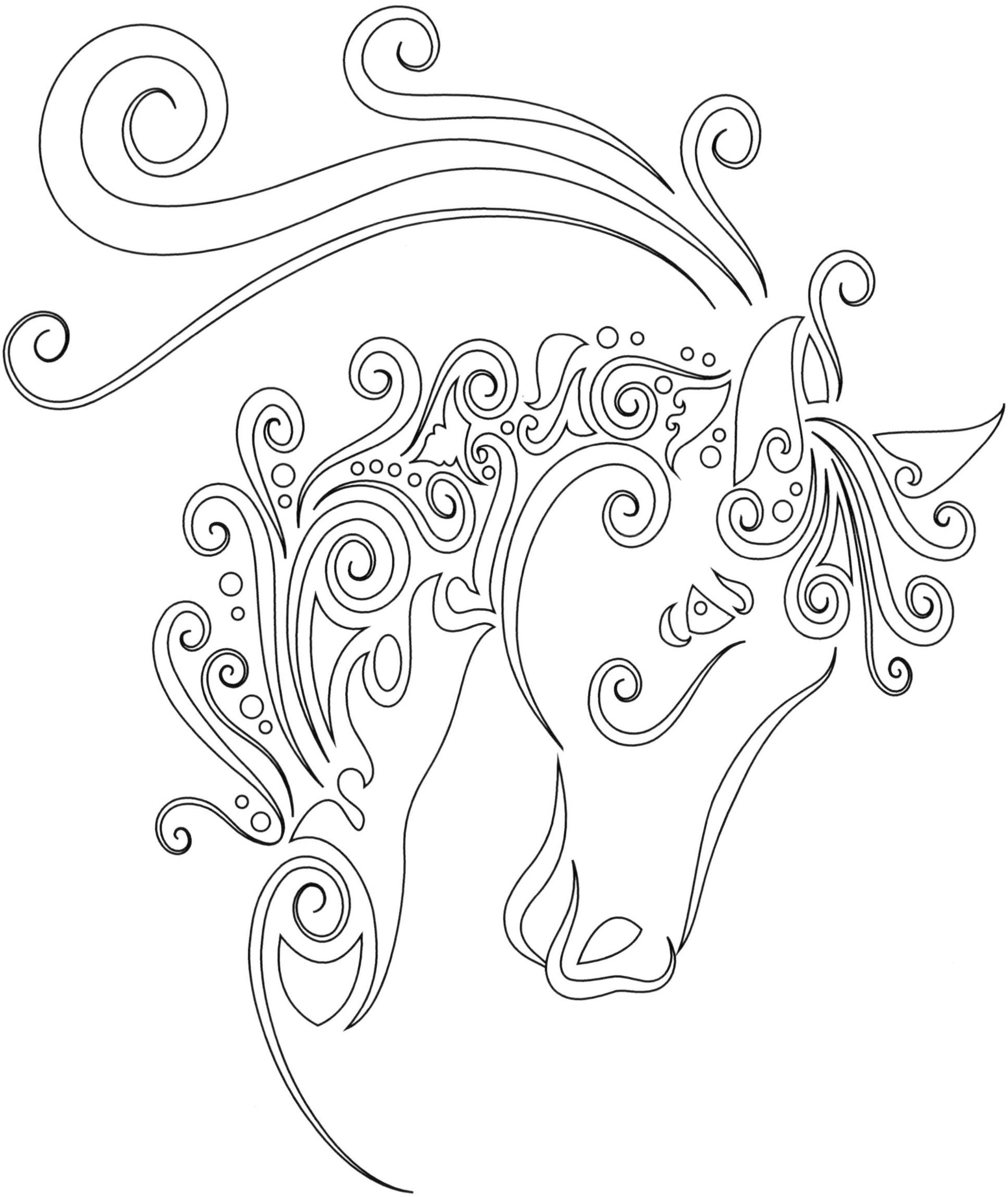

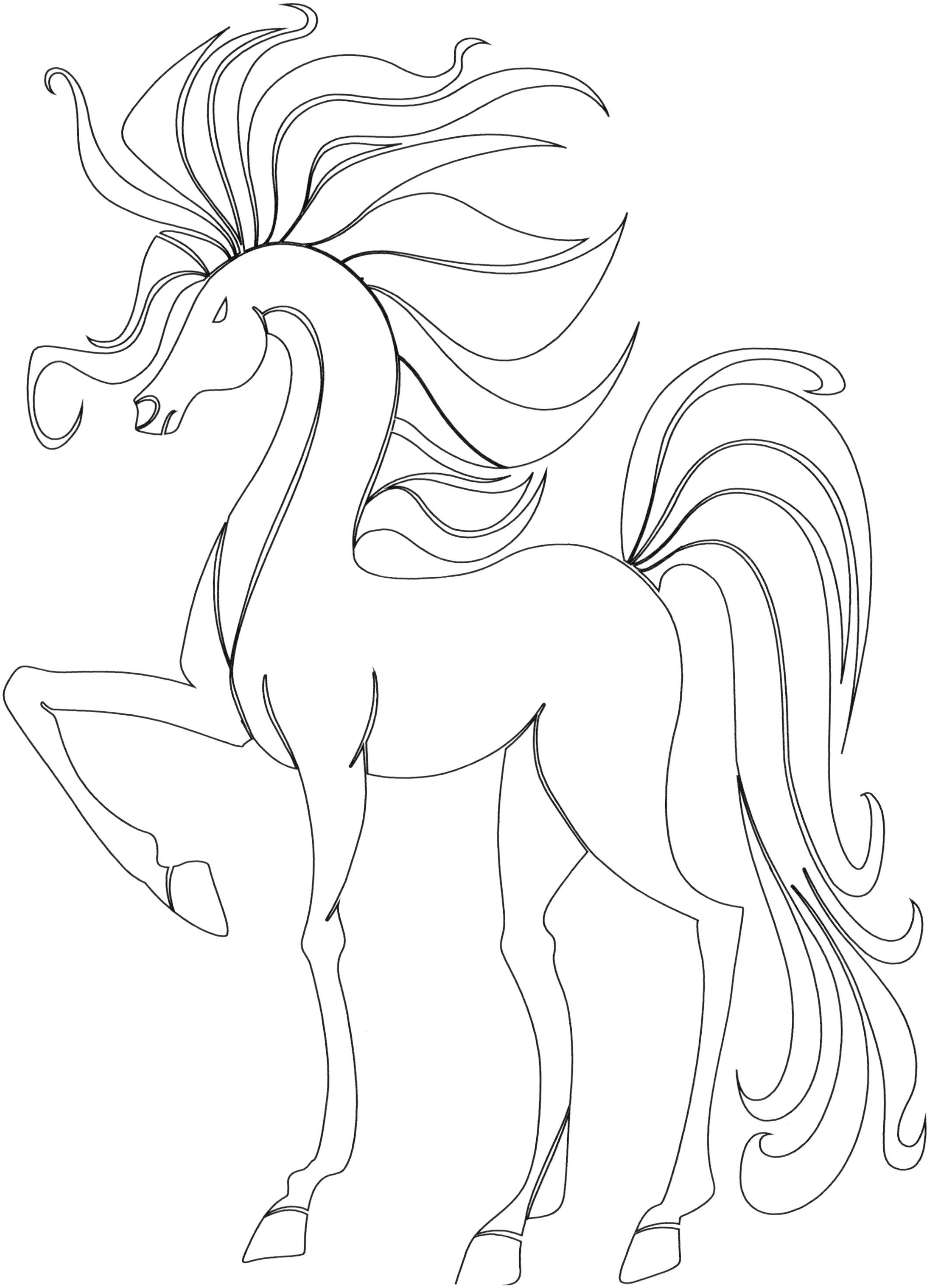

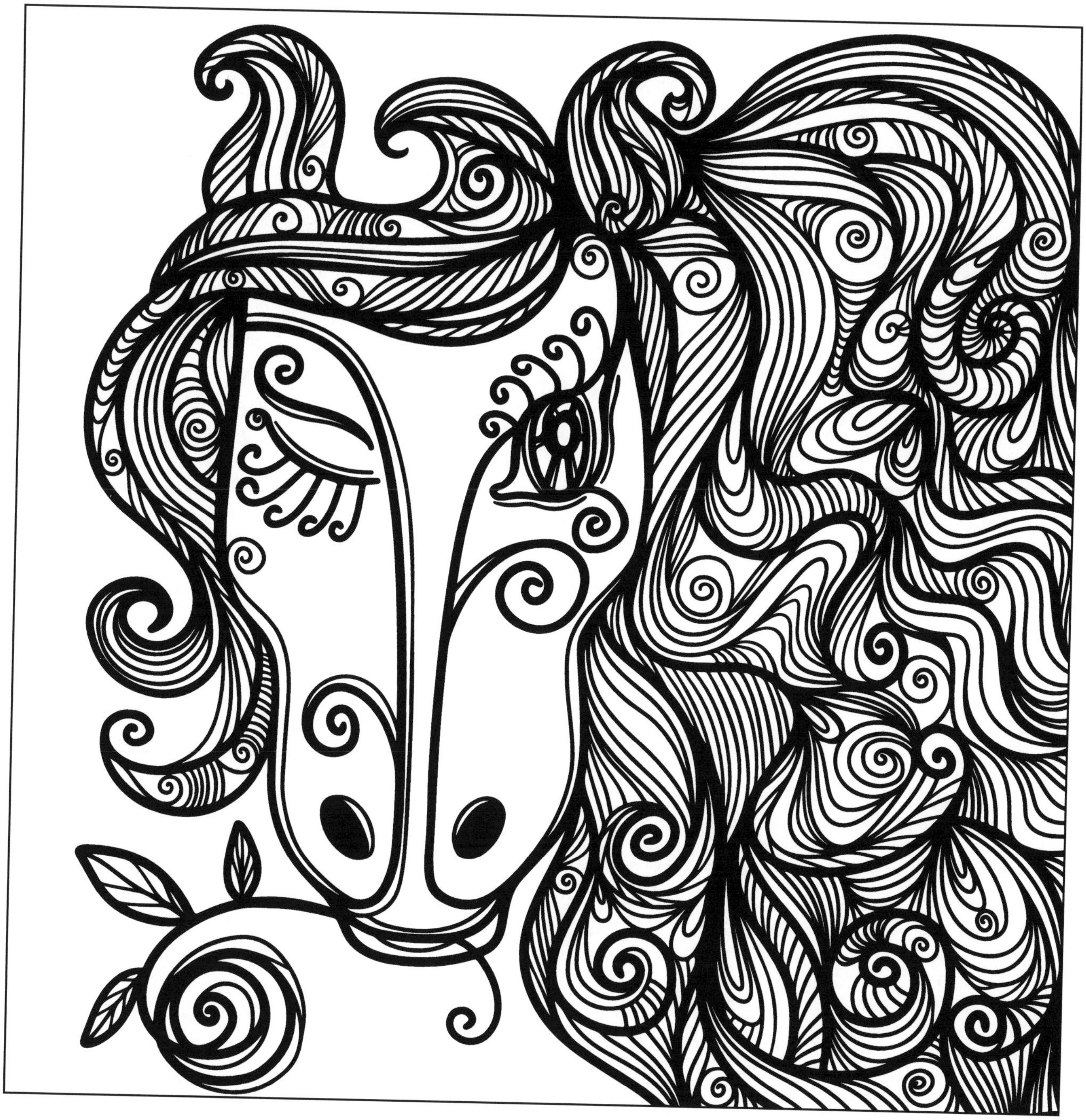

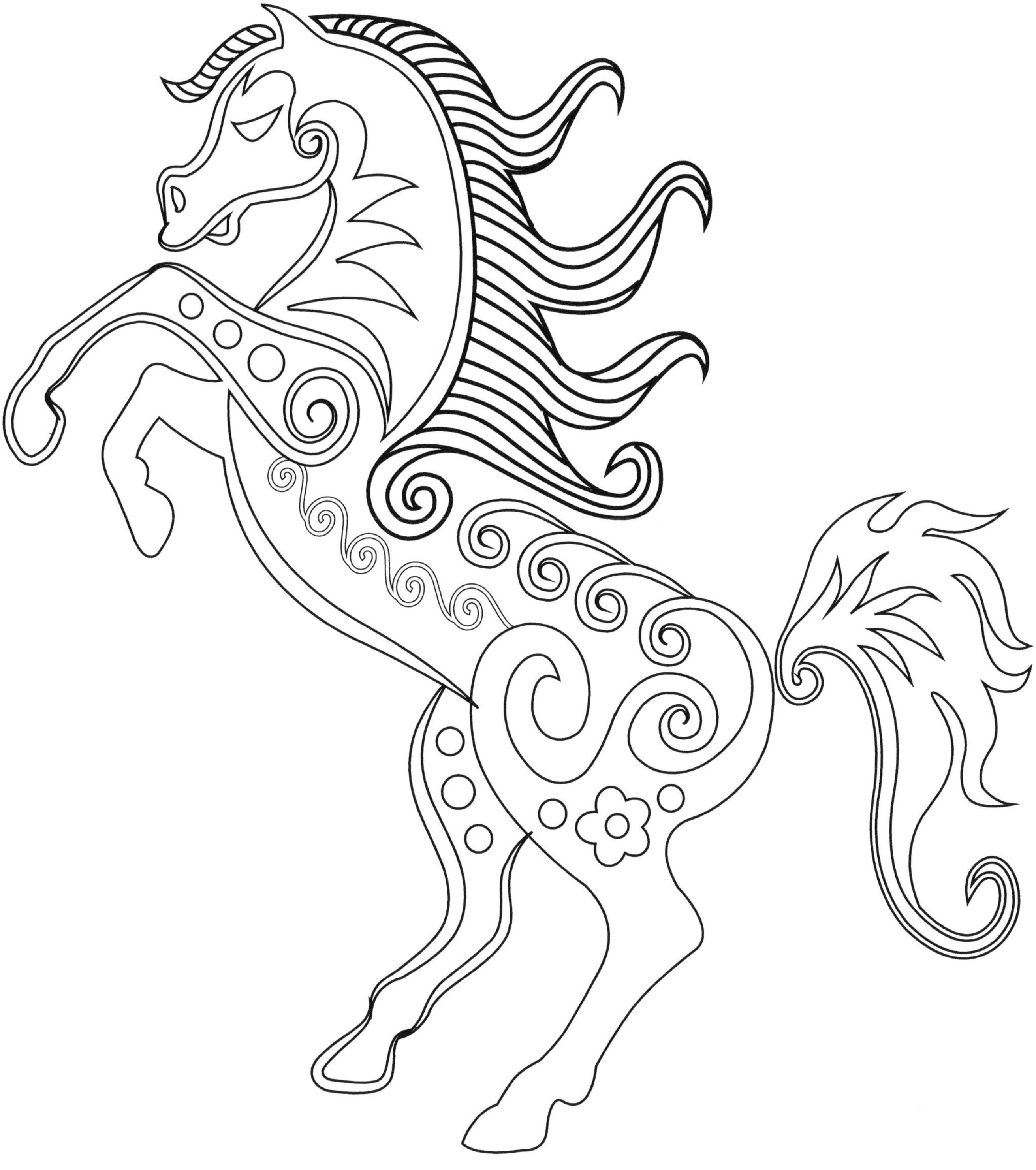

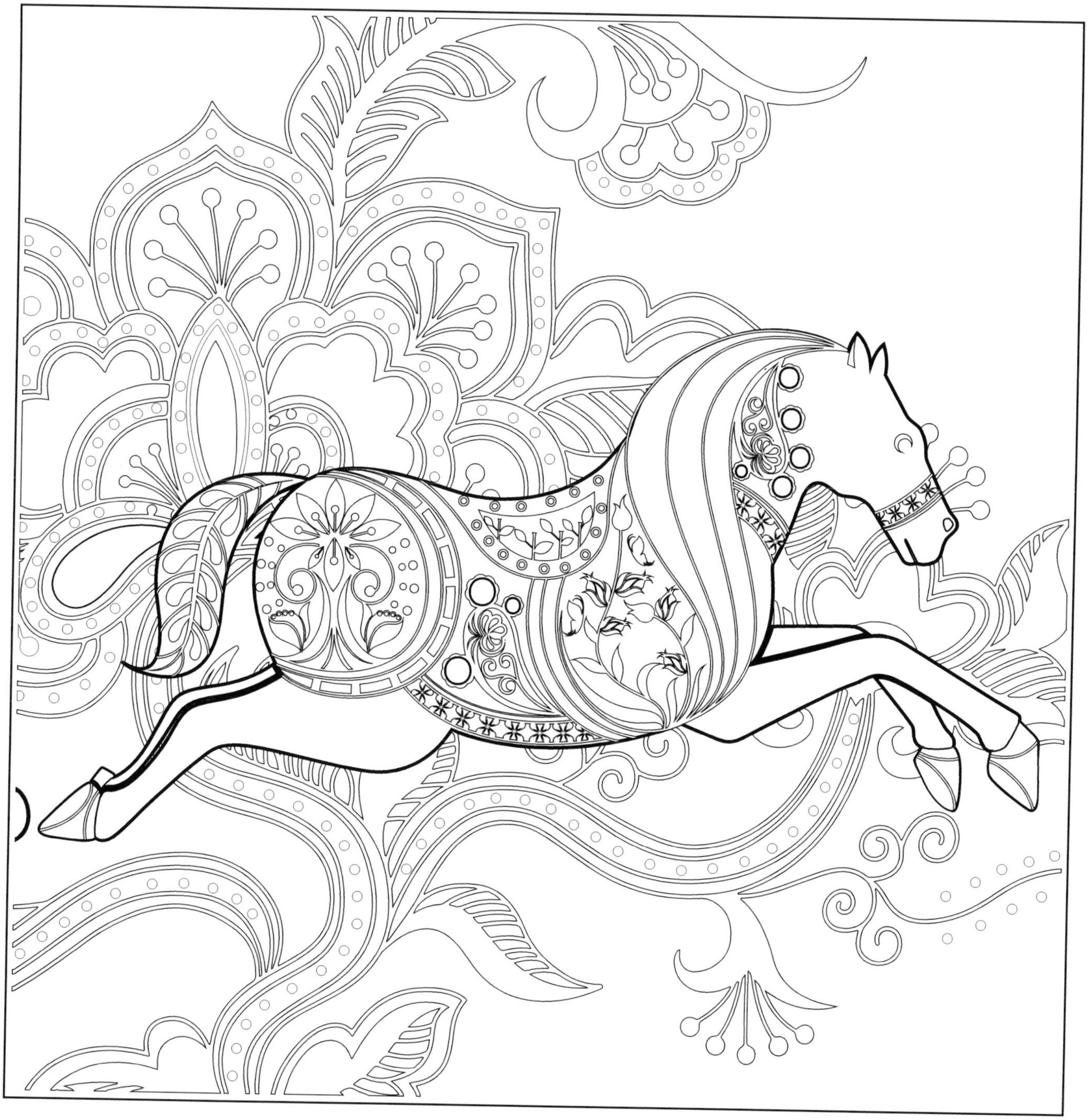

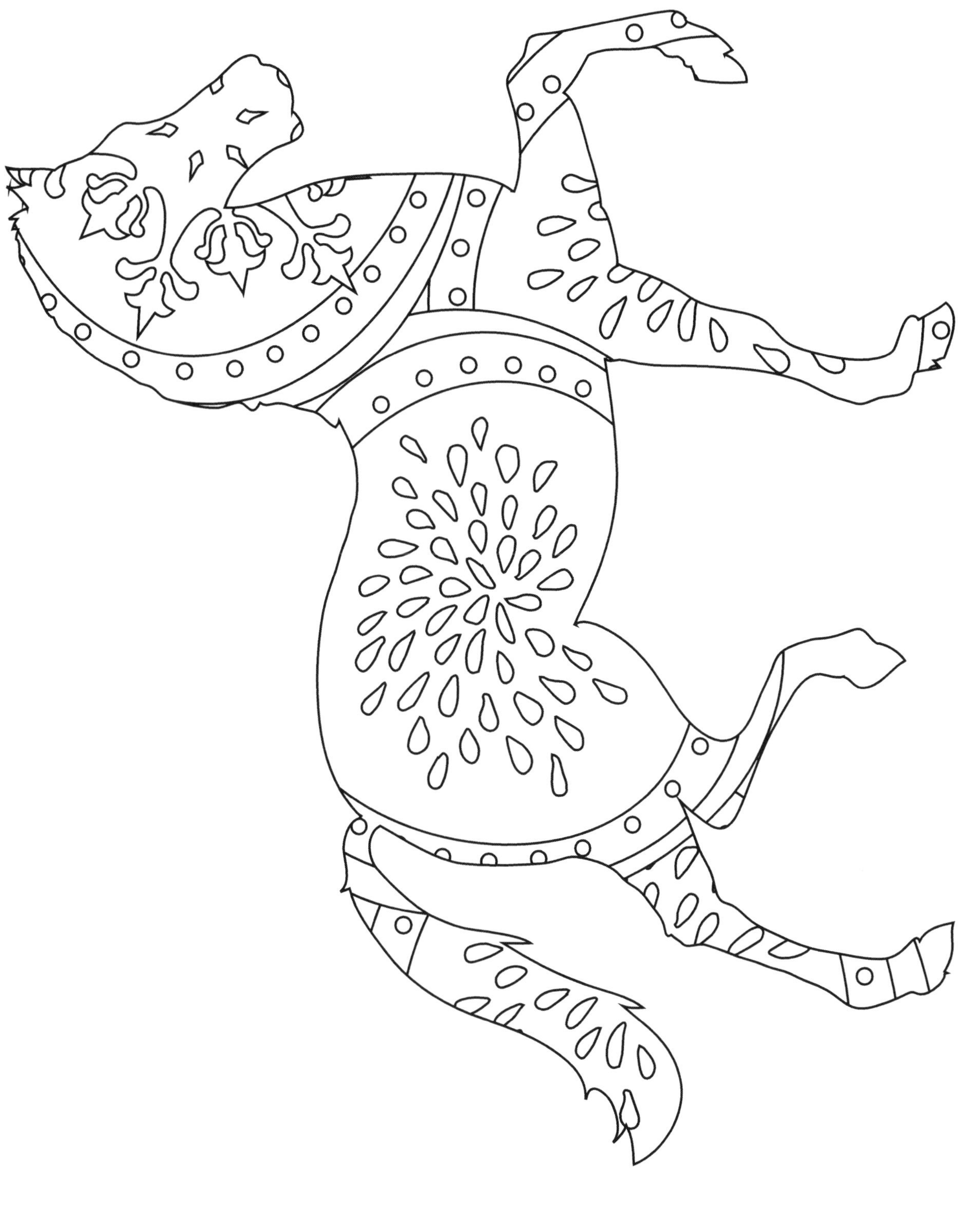

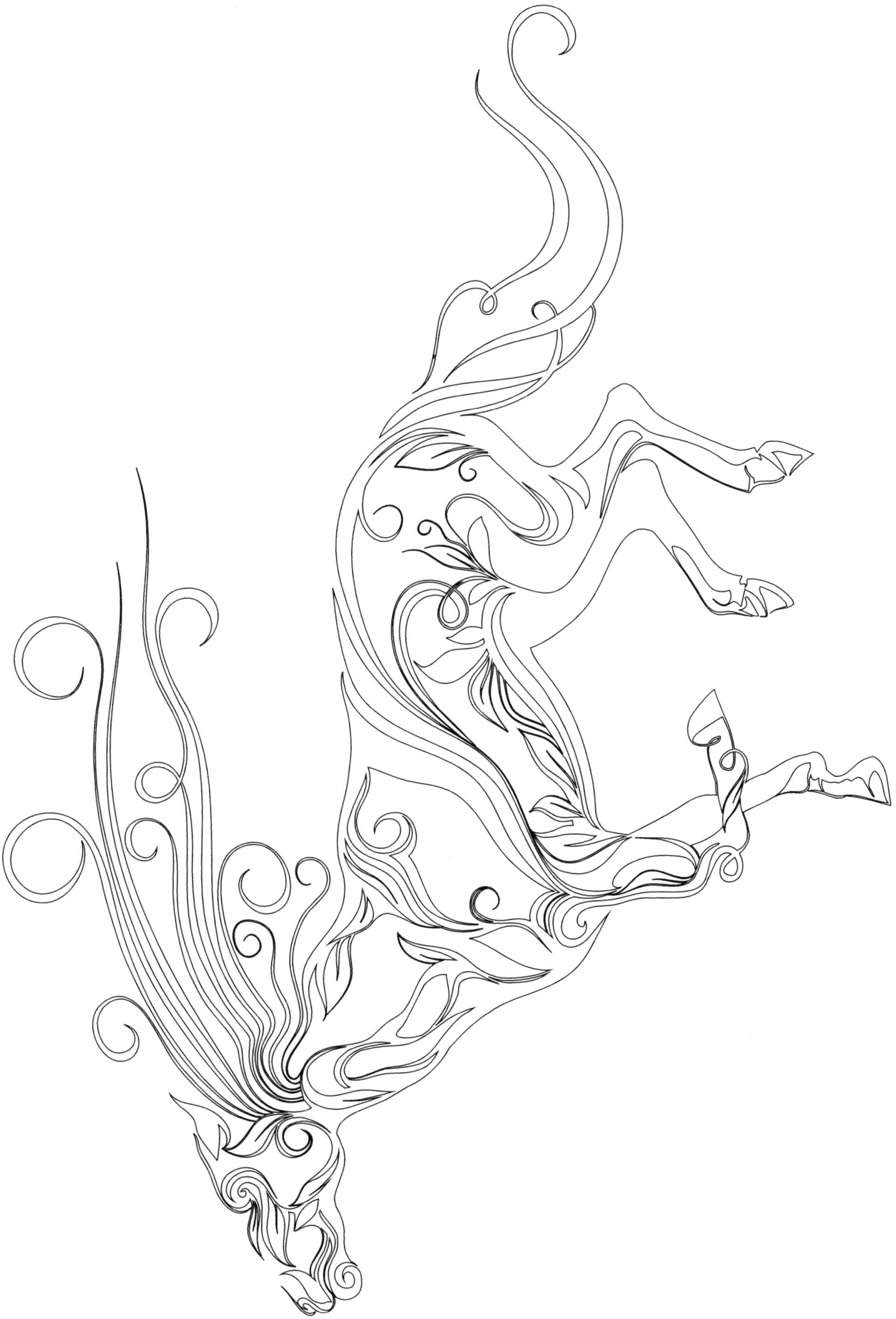

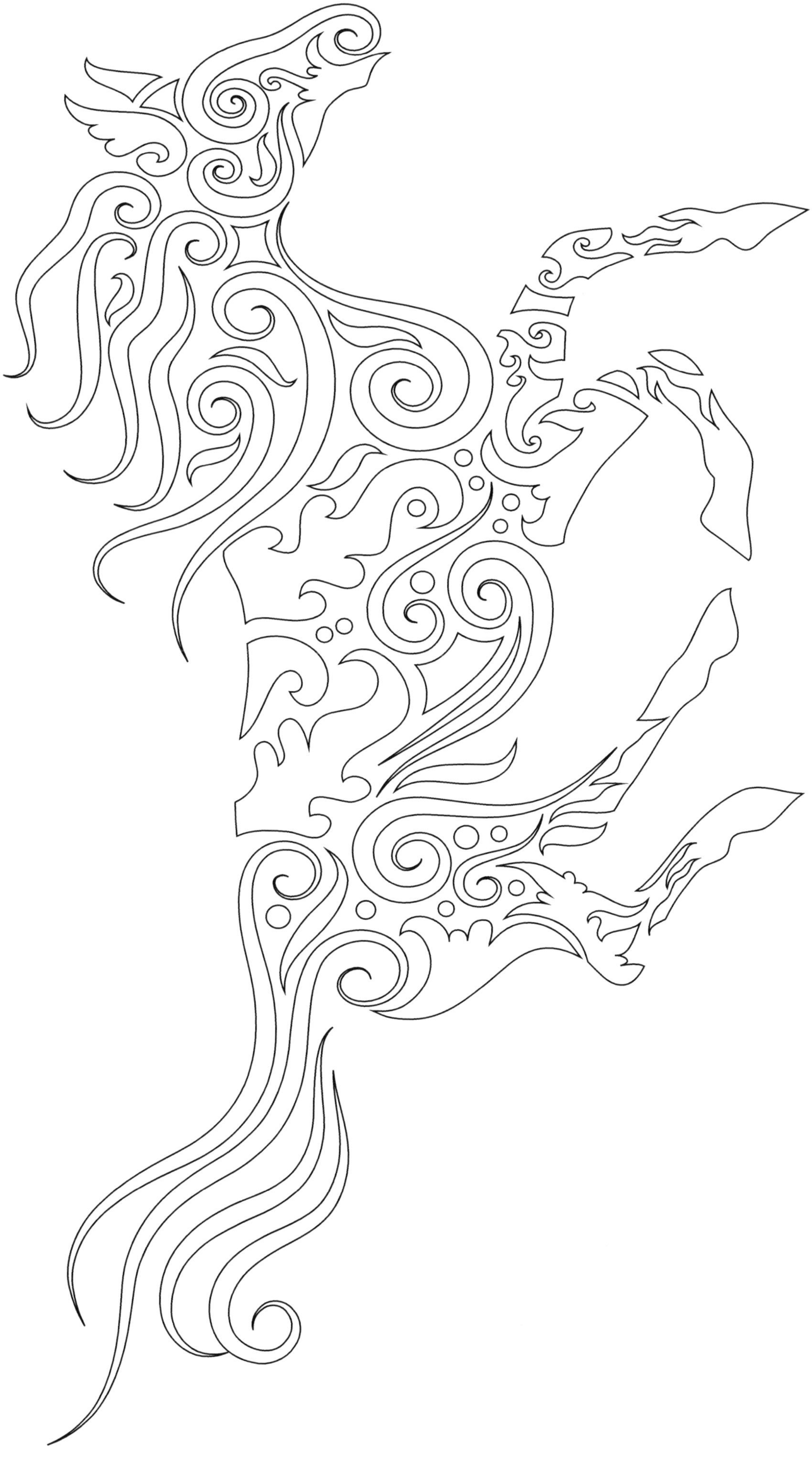

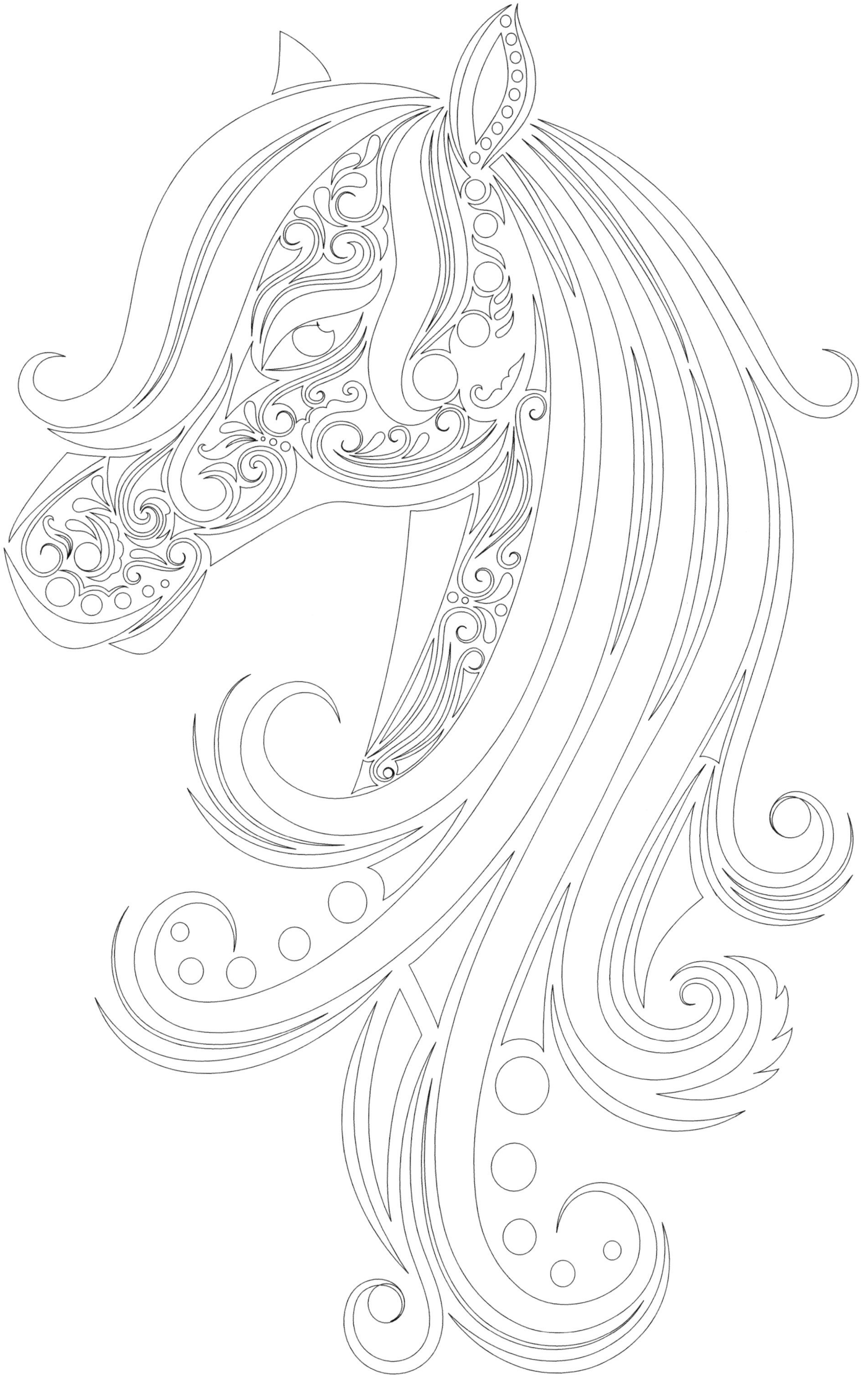

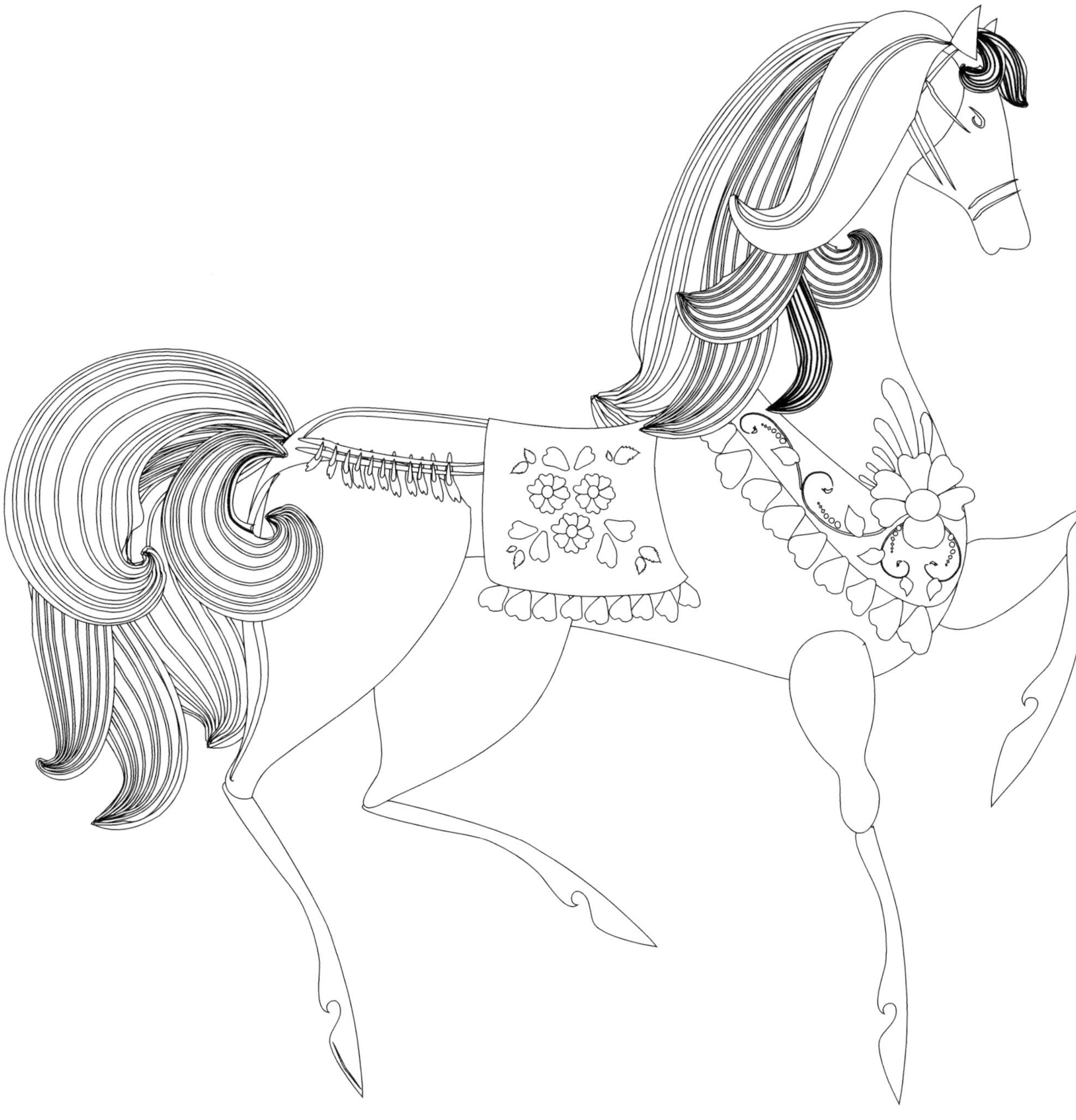

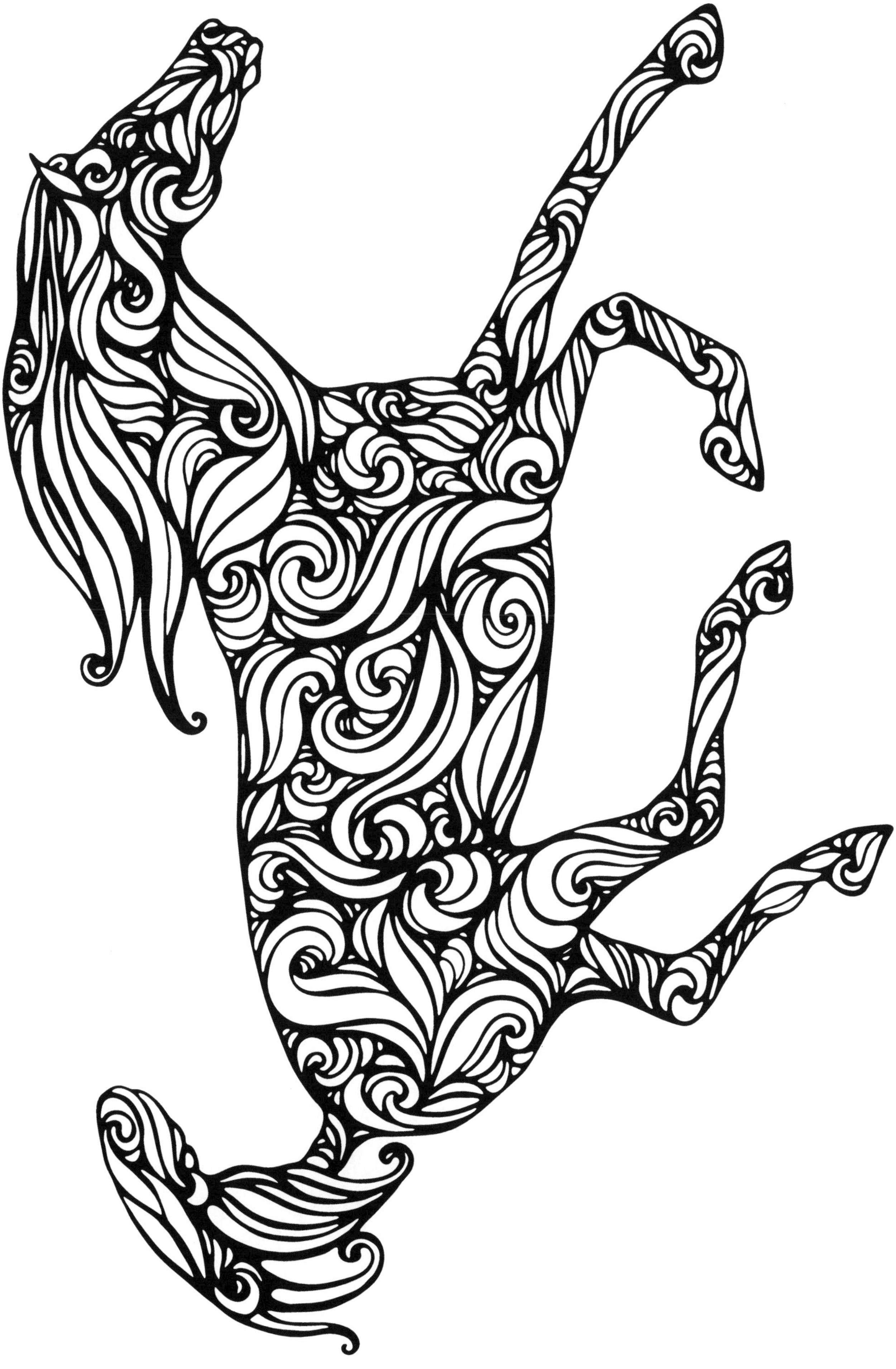

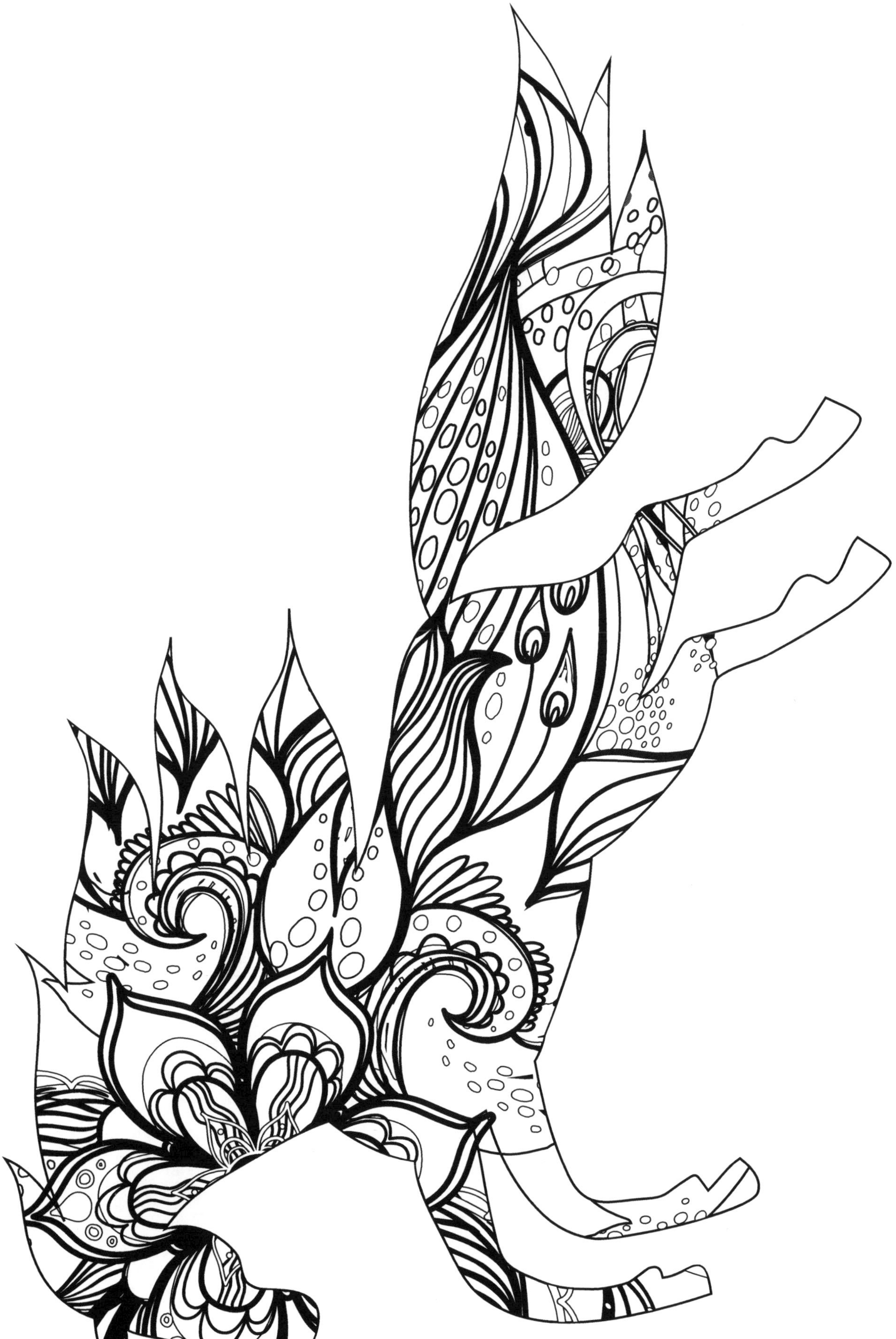

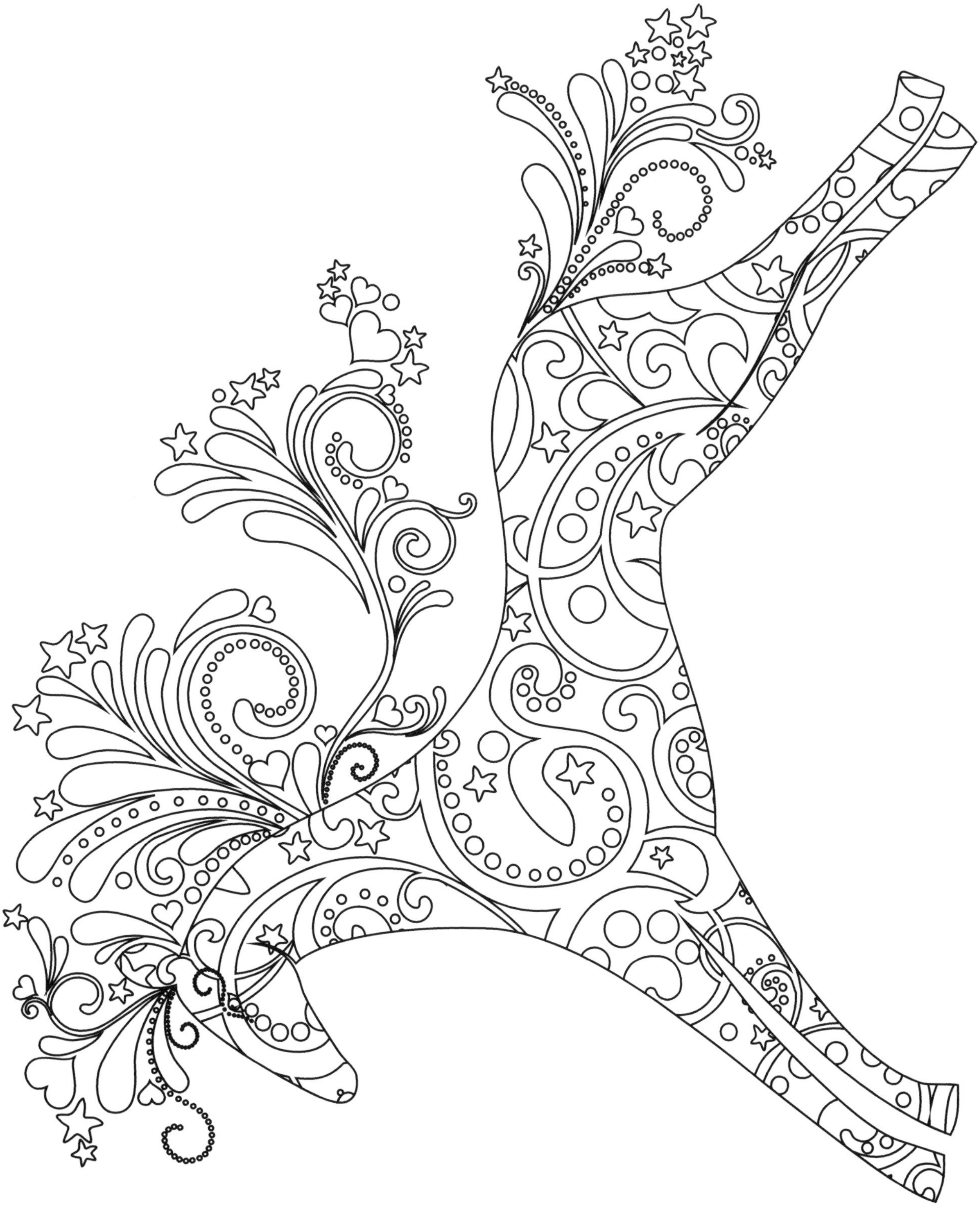

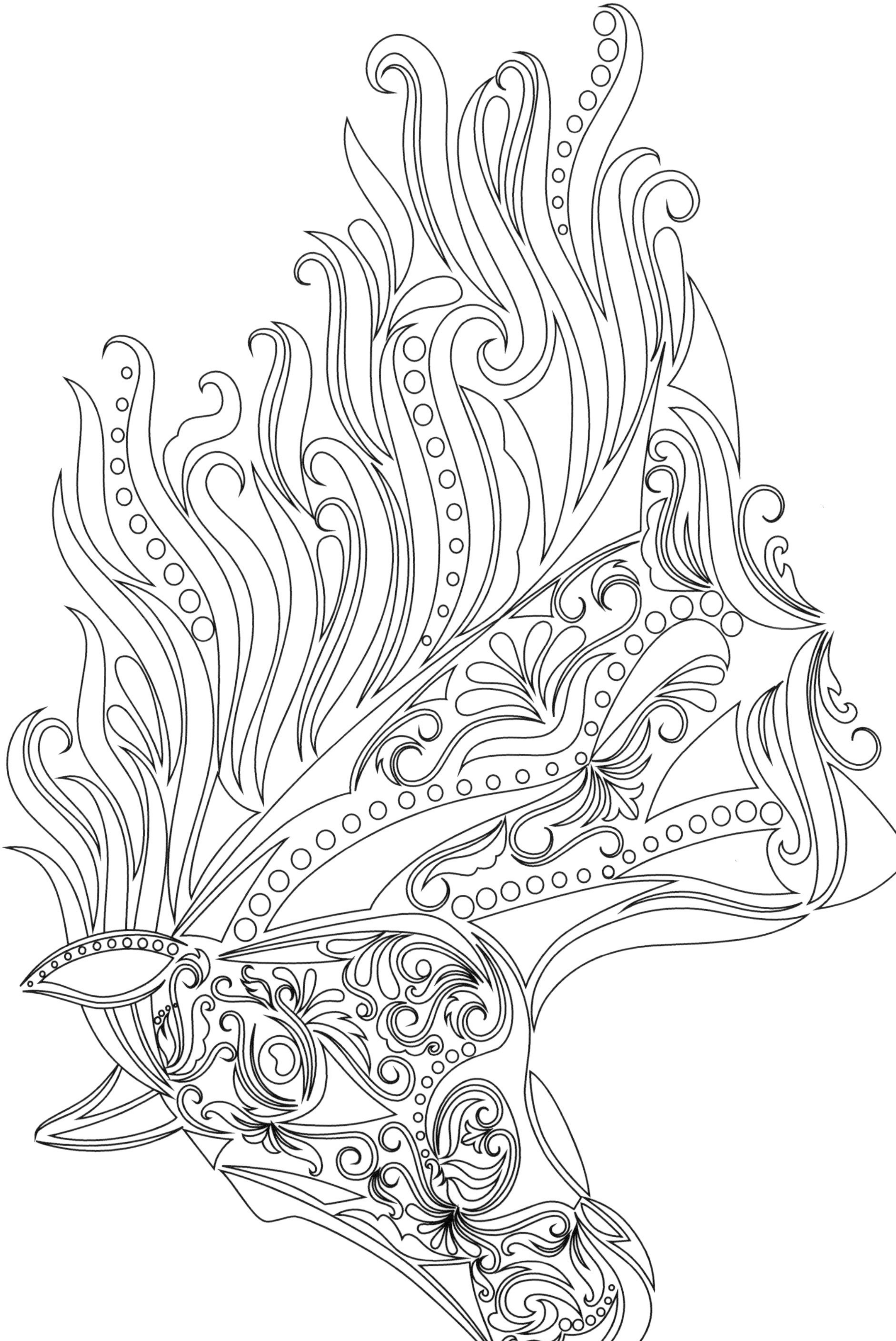

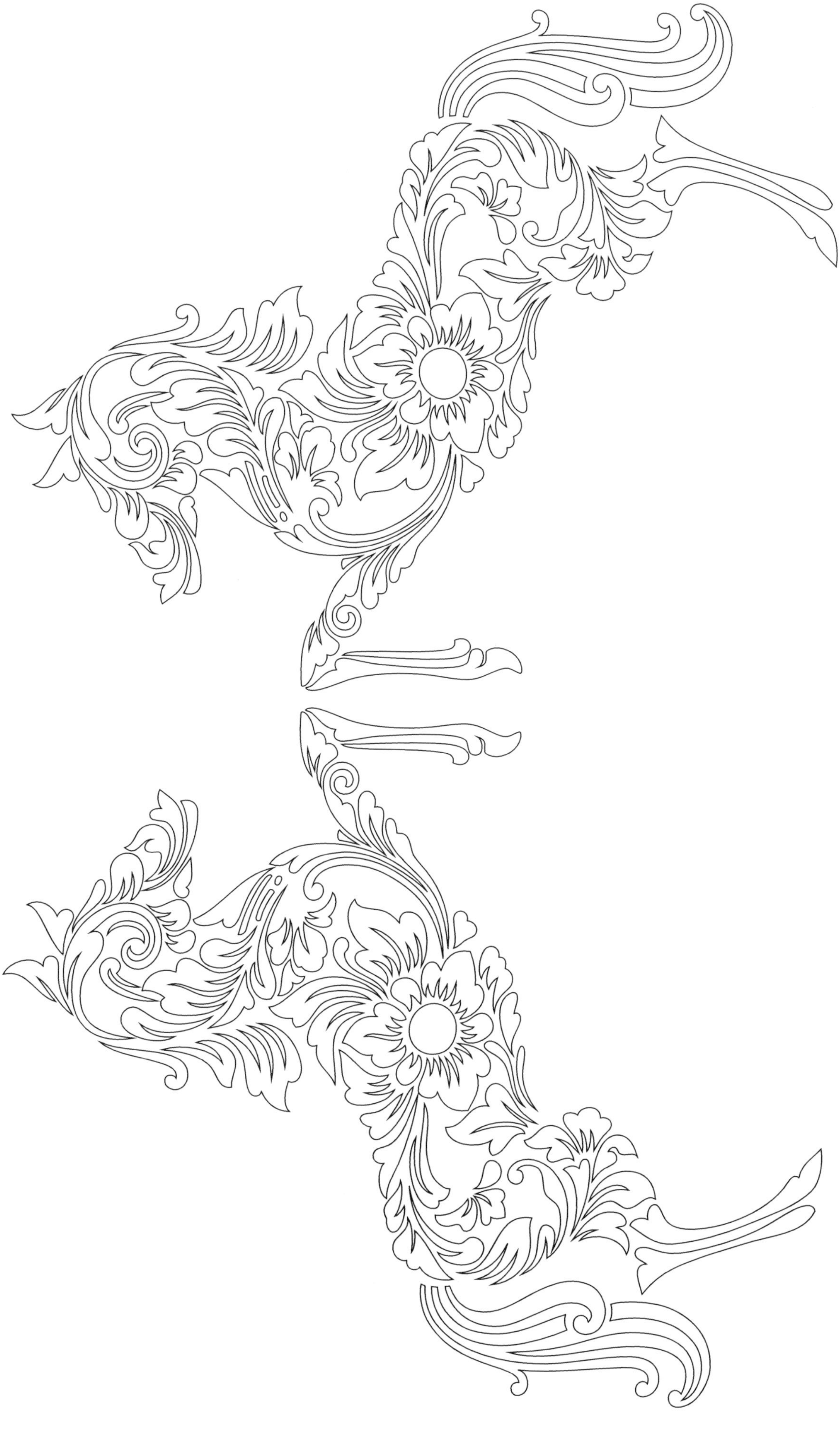

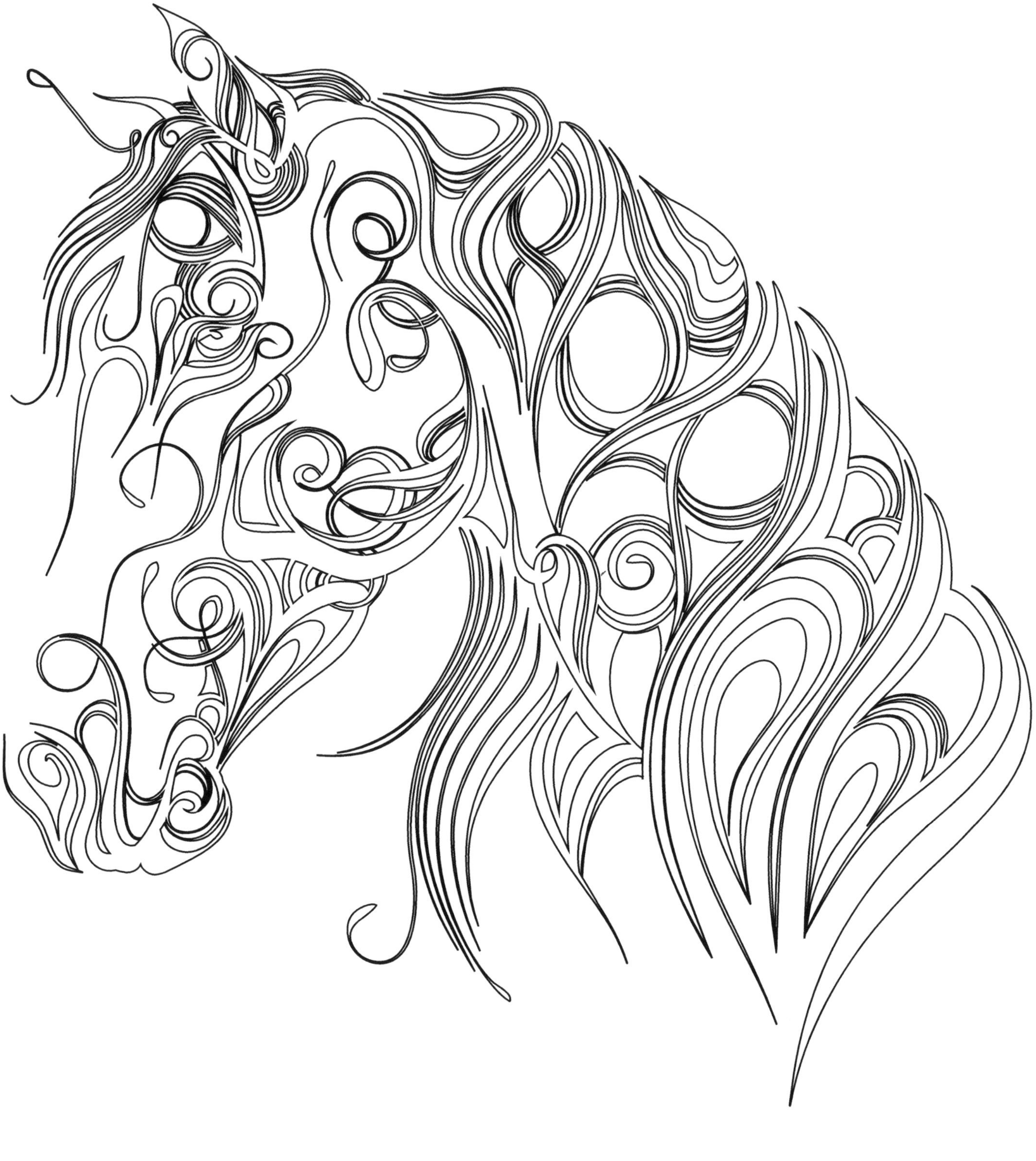

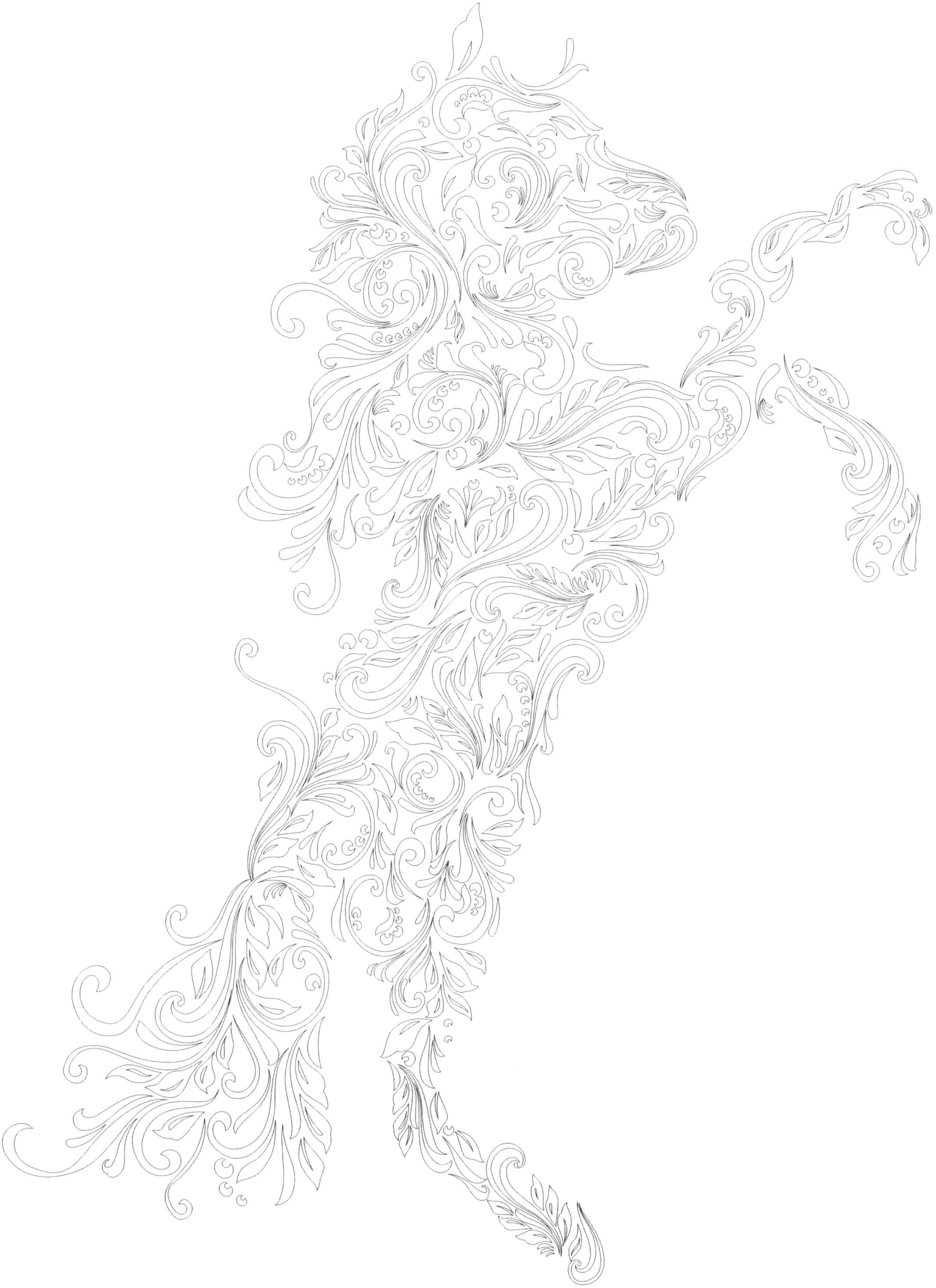

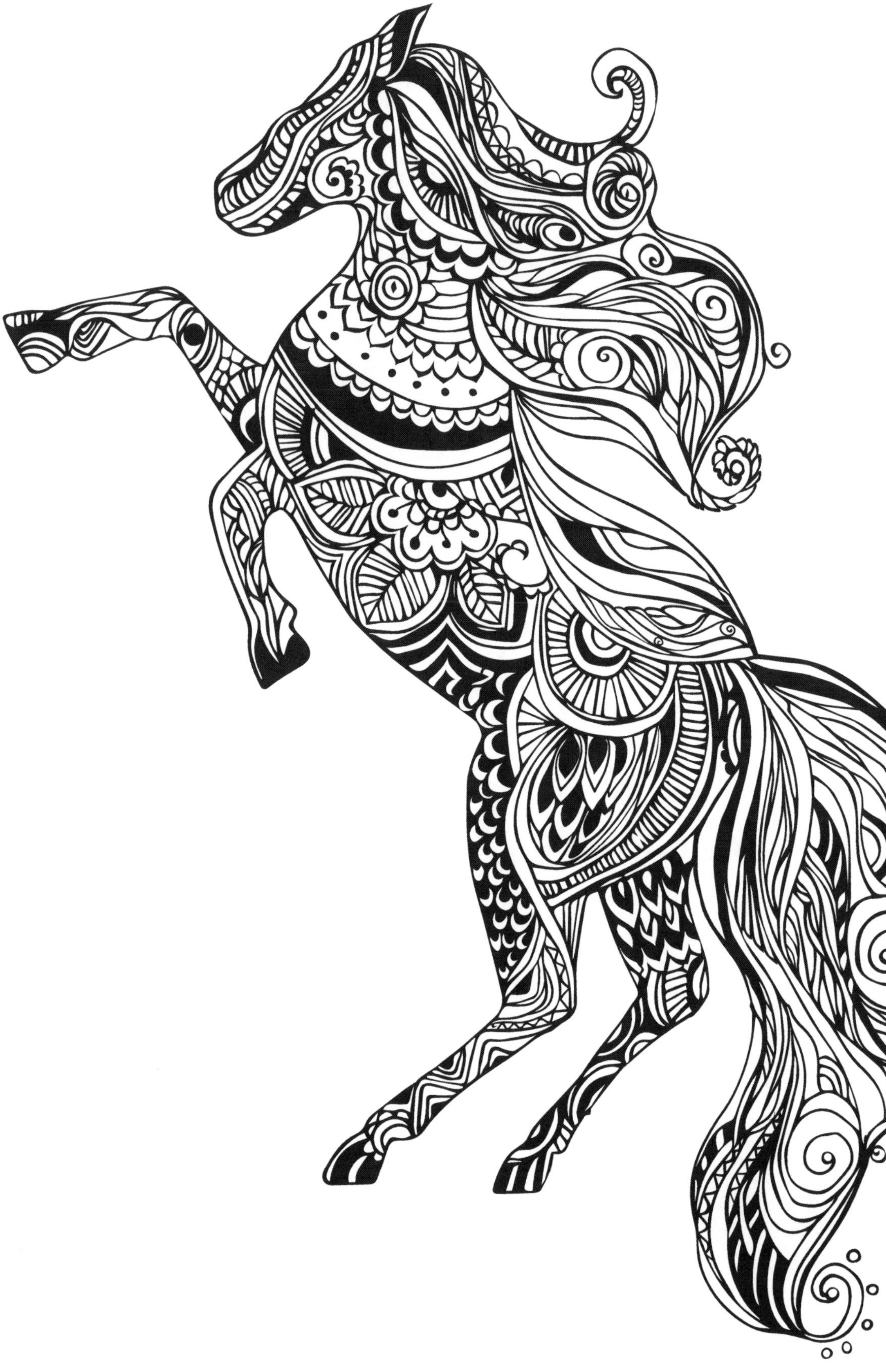

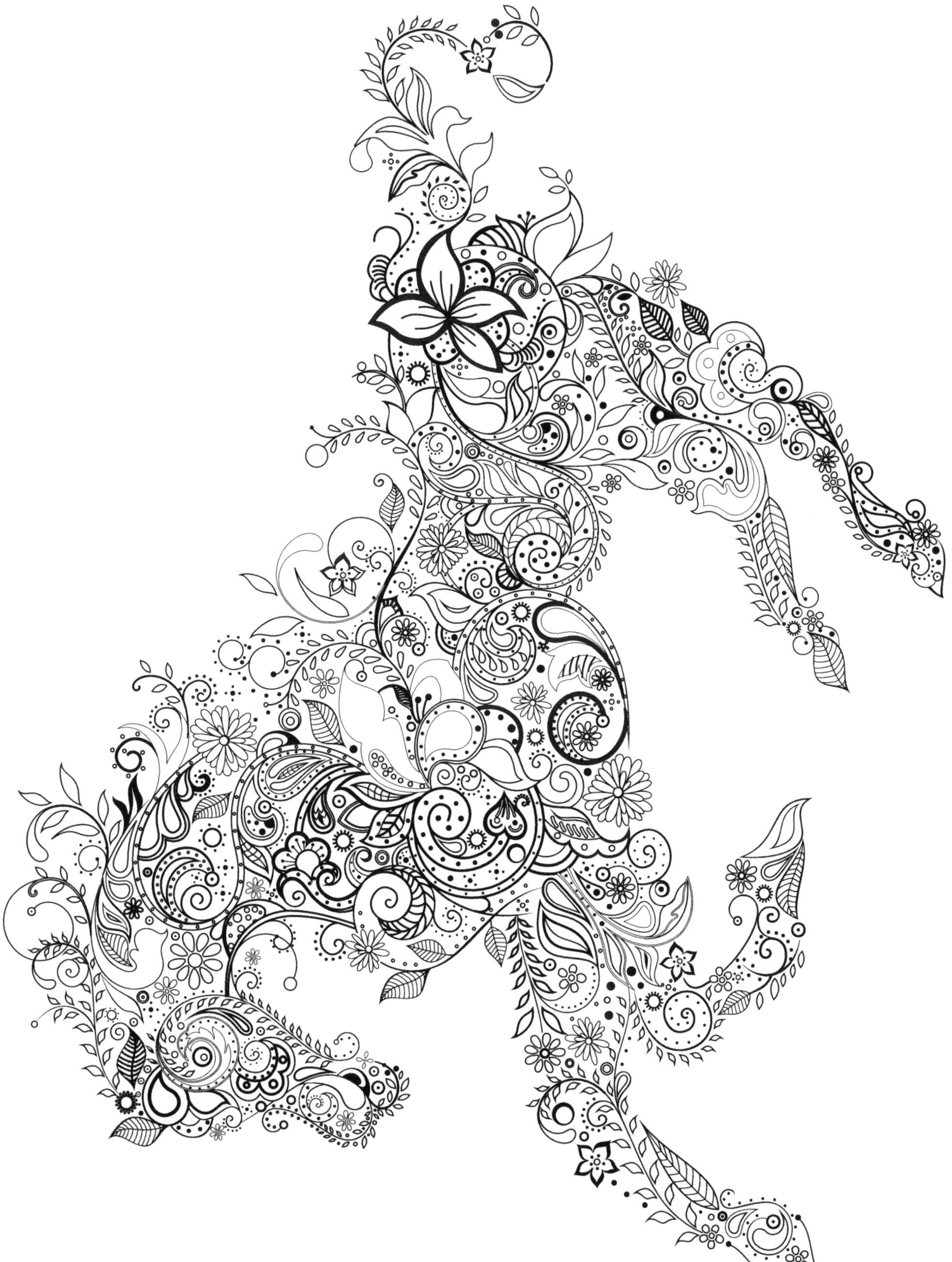

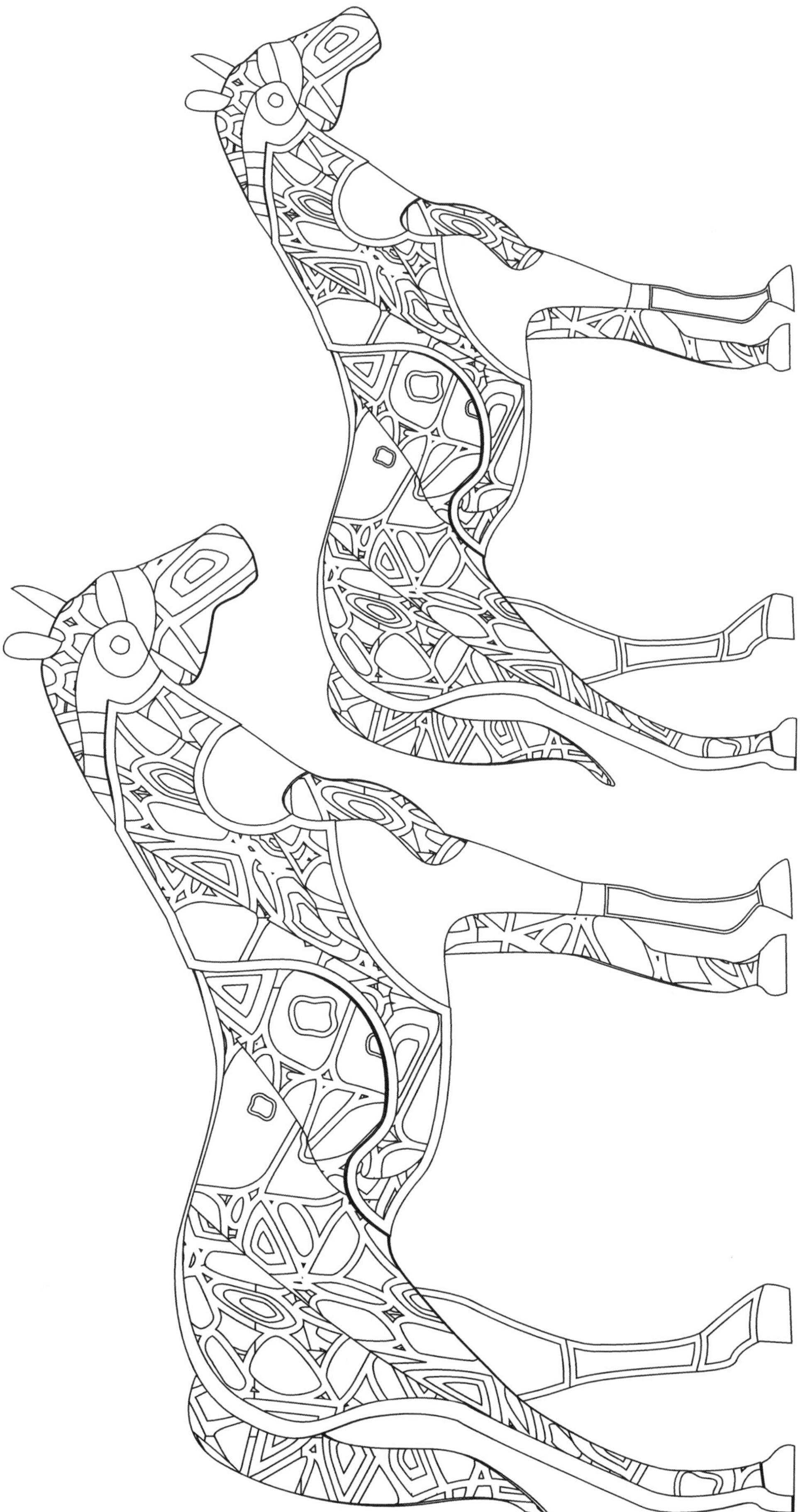

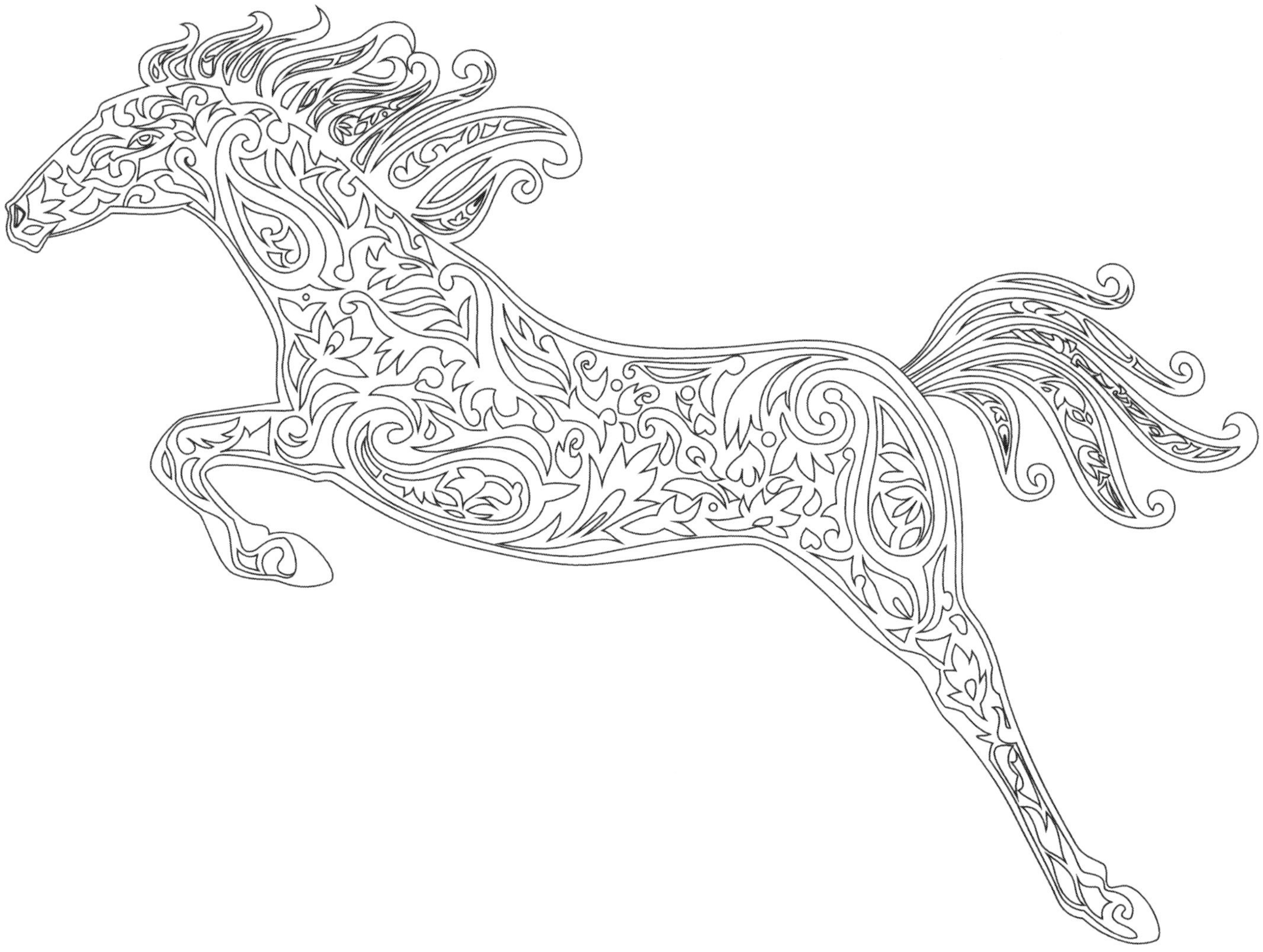

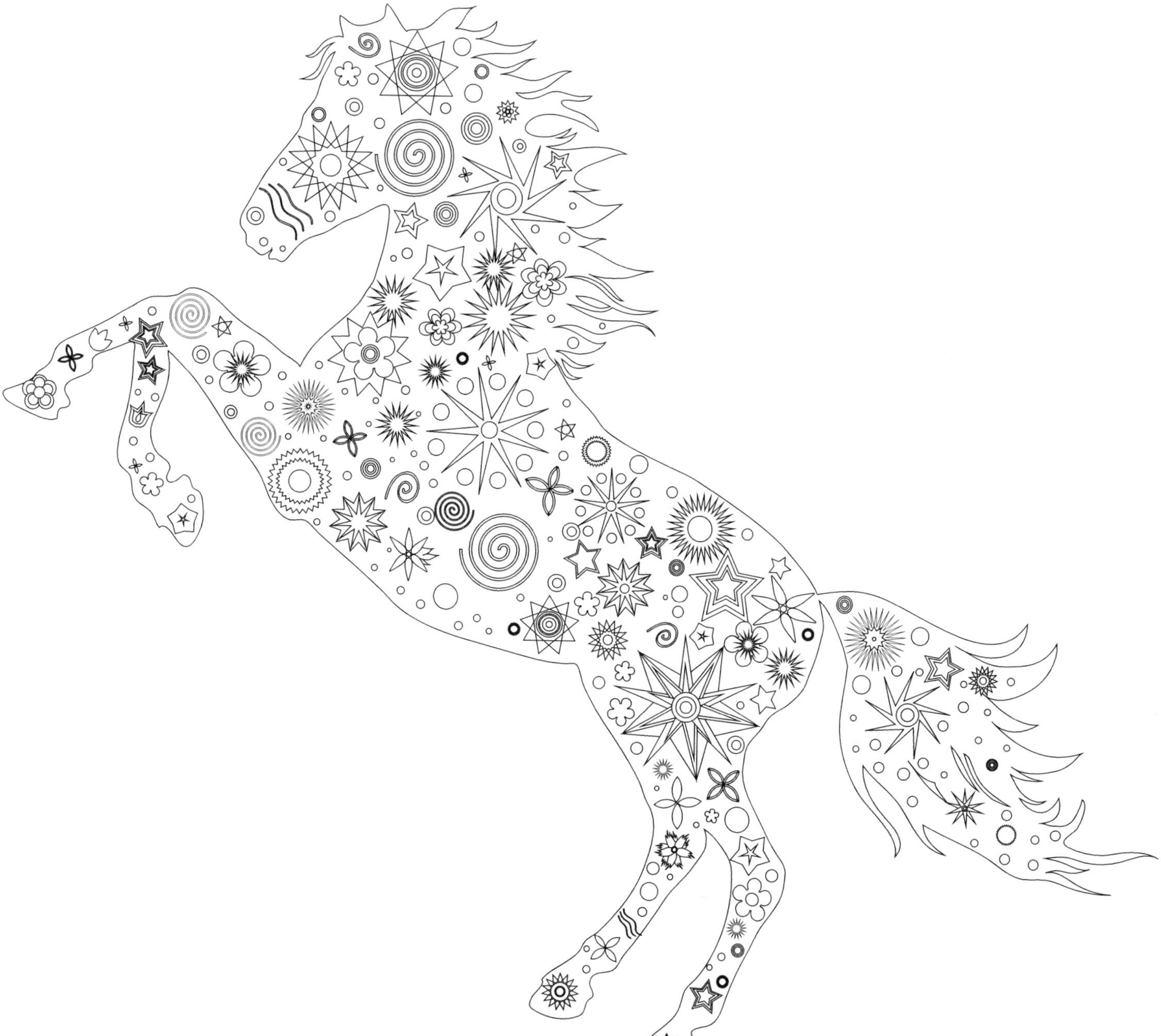

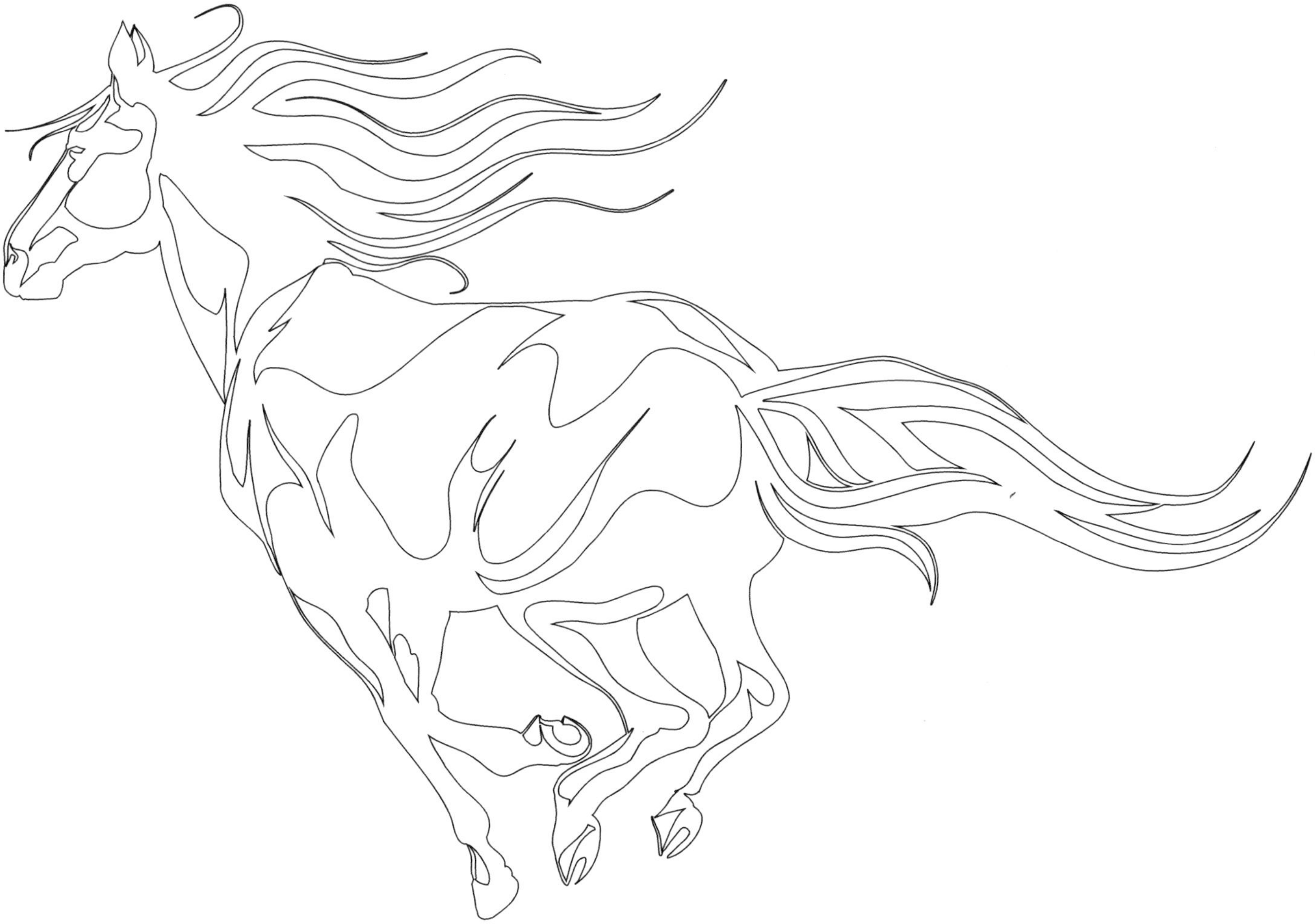

55604235R00031

Made in the USA
Middletown, DE
11 December 2017